Under Your Feet

by Joanne Ryder

illustrated by Dennis Nolan

Four Winds Press

New York

For Marilyn and Morris Sachs,
dear friends and joyful walkers — J.R.

For Colleen, Gary, and Don
and memories of home — D.N.

Special thanks to Dr. Ann Squire, curator of education,
Central Park Zoo, for her expert reading of the manuscript.

Printed and bound in Japan. First American Edition   10 9 8 7 6 5 4 3 2 1

The text of this book is set in 14 point ITC Garamond Book Condensed.
The illustrations are rendered in watercolor.

Library of Congress Cataloging-in-Publication Data • Ryder, Joanne. Under your feet/
Joanne Ryder; illustrated by Dennis Nolan. — 1st American ed.   p.   cm.
Summary: A collection of poems about nature and wildlife, spanning all the seasons of the year.
ISBN 0-02-777955-6
1. Nature — Juvenile poetry. 2. Seasons — Juvenile poetry. 3. Children's poetry, American.
[1. Nature — Poetry. 2. Seasons — Poetry. 3. American poetry.] I. Nolan, Dennis, ill. II. Title.
PS3568.Y399U5   1990   811′ .54 — dc20   89-33897   CIP   AC

Under the ground
under the grass
under your feet
creatures are hiding.
Tucked in the earth
or deep in the pond,
hidden by leaves or ice,
small creatures live nearby.

You can listen,
but you may not hear their voices.
You can look,
but you may not see them moving.
Yet they are there.
Try and see
if you can feel them.

When the snows melt
and the frozen ground thaws,
open your window wide
and smell spring
as the soft wet earth
warms in the sun.
The sun warms you, too,
as you walk over ground
no longer stiff and hard,
over earth that crumbles
under your feet.

Spring touches others —
toads underground
stretch their strong legs;
snakes buried deep
uncurl and slide
through the damp soil;
turtles kick and kick,
their short legs
churning, pushing
them upward.

Can you feel the sleepers
waking, stretching, rising
through the dark earth
up to the sun?

Soon spring green
creeps everywhere—
pale green leaves
brighten the trees,
fuzzy grass covers the ground.
A brown furry mole
as big as your hand
digs long narrow tunnels
just under the grass roots.
Quickly she catches worms
wriggling above her,
falling into her home.
Under the new grass
soft furry mole eats her breakfast
and purrs!

Spring makes you want
to run and run
in the short green grass.
    Can you feel
    a sleek lively mole
    racing with you,
    running through her home
    below your feet?

White petals
float down
like late spring snow
on a thick green carpet.
Someone new
peeks out
from a dark tunnel
into the sun.
A young woodchuck
with tiny bright eyes
watches new things —
shadows flickering;
petals drifting down;
you, passing by.
    Can you feel him
    watching you,
    wondering
    what you might be?

On hot summer days,
you run from the sun,
dive into the pond.
Cold water surrounds you,
then trickles down
your smooth wet skin.

Fish darts deeper,
feeling the water tremble
against her silver scales,
feeling you kick and kick
your way across the surface.
   And when you rest,
   floating quietly,
   can you feel
   the quiet swimmer
   circling slowly
   in the cool water below?

As you climb the muddy bank,
your foot touches
a small hole underwater,
muskrat's doorway.
His tunnel leads up
through the mud
to his dry den
under the ground
under the grass.
Inside his home,
muskrat stretches
after his long day's nap.
While you walk away,
leaving muddy footprints
on the grass above,
he runs down
through his dark tunnel
and into the calm water.
    Can you feel
    muskrat's ripples
    tickling the pond?

Just before sunset
you find a good place to rest,
a big flat rock shaded by trees.
You listen to water
trickling over stones
and wait for the hot day to end.
Under the rock
a salamander waits, too,
curled around her eggs,
keeping them safe
so the young ones
curled inside can grow.
　　Can you feel
　　her waiting
　　with you
　　as the summer sun sinks
　　behind the trees?

The long long grass
bends and rises,
dancing in the cool wind.
Far below
cricket waits
in his cave under a stone.
Soon he will creep out,
soon he will
scrape his wings,
making night music.
As you push your way
through grass thigh high,
cricket feels
the ground around him
shake and shake.
     Can you feel him
     waiting till you pass,
     waiting in the darkness,
     full of song?

Like chilly mornings,
fall apples taste sharp and cool.
Your fingers slide
around the smooth bright ball.
Your tongue tingles
with the juicy taste of fall.

Bright scraps of leaves
land everywhere and
crackle under your feet.
Nearby, leaves whisper
as someone makes a trail
beneath the leafy carpet
to the old damp log
where snails cling,
hiding from the light.

Tiny shrew
crunches a hard shell
and bites into softness.
    Can you hear her
    eating her meal
    under the golden leaves?

One gray day
you can hear autumn
honking across the sky.
You see winter
rising from chimneys
in dark gray puffs.
Now the world seems quiet,
everyone seems far away
but you.

In the cold earth
toads sleep, frogs hush,
turtles tuck themselves
inside their shells.
Deep down,
woodchuck rests,
but mole stays awake,
digging her way
through winter.
   Can you feel
   mole digging
   deeper and deeper
   under your feet?

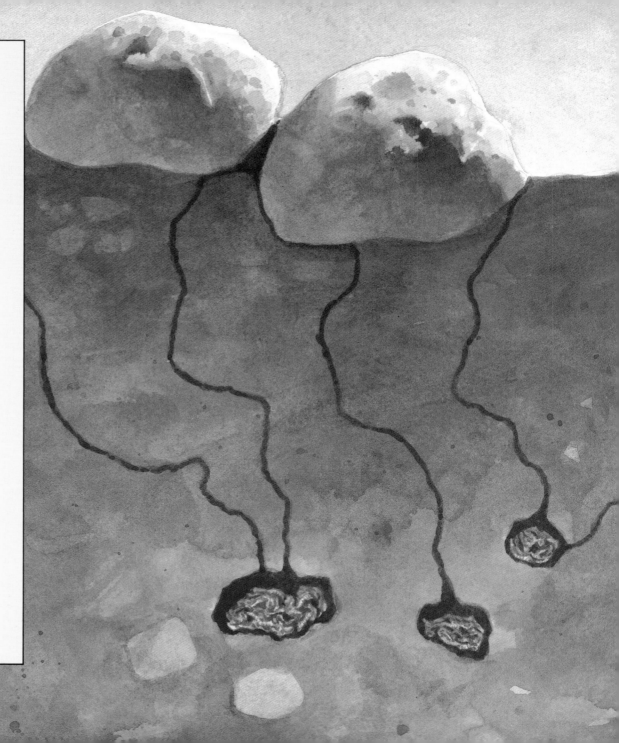

When you face winter,
you wrap yourself in wool,
tuck feet in boots
and fingers in mittens.
But winter always wins,
chasing you to someplace warm.

Even worms
feel winter chasing them
and wriggle away,
making tunnels down
to warmer places
where they meet
and rest.

Thousands of worms
huddle in balls
deep in the ground,
breathing quietly
through their soft skins.
    Can you feel them
    resting
    safe and warm
    all winter long?

You pick icicles
from the gray branches.
As you walk with care
around the frozen pond,
your breath chills white
in front of you.

Under a white roof of ice,
otter swims,
streams of bubbles
trailing behind.
He dives down,
looking for
slow-moving fish
in the dark cold waters,
and dives up,
out of breath.
Can you feel
otter breathing,
filling his lungs
with good cold air
trapped in a bubble
under the ice?

One bitter morning
coldness wakes you
and you burrow
under your covers,
waiting and wondering
when the cold will end.

Outside
under piles of snow
under the hard ground
in snug nests
of grass and leaves,
jumping mice sleep
tucked tight
in fat furry balls.
    Can you feel
    them dreaming
    of warm spring nights
    when they'll leap
    through the
    grassy field again?

From year to year,
you live and grow
between earth and sky.
Here is your home.
Others live here, too.
They are near,
all around you,
sharing this place
with you.

Can you feel them?